AI WORLD
AI AT HOME

by Ford Chambers

pogo

Ideas for Parents and Teachers

Pogo Books let children practice reading informational text while introducing them to nonfiction features such as headings, labels, sidebars, maps, and diagrams, as well as a table of contents, glossary, and index.

Carefully leveled text with a strong photo match offers early fluent readers the support they need to succeed.

Before Reading

- "Walk" through the book and point out the various nonfiction features. Ask the student what purpose each feature serves.
- Look at the glossary together. Read and discuss the words.

Read the Book

- Have the child read the book independently.
- Invite them to list questions that arise from reading.

After Reading

- Discuss the child's questions. Talk about how they might find answers to those questions.
- Prompt the child to think more. Ask: Do you have AI in your home? Would you like to? Why or why not?

Pogo Books are published by Jump!
5357 Penn Avenue South
Minneapolis, MN 55419
www.jumplibrary.com

Copyright © 2025 Jump!
International copyright reserved in all countries. No part of this book may be reproduced in any form without written permission from the publisher.

Library of Congress Cataloging-in-Publication Data

Names: Chambers, Ford, author.
Title: AI at home / by Ford Chambers.
Description: Minneapolis, MN: Jump!, Inc., [2025]
Series: AI world | Includes index.
Audience: Ages 7-10
Identifiers: LCCN 2024023292 (print)
LCCN 2024023293 (ebook)
ISBN 9798892135535 (hardcover)
ISBN 9798892135542 (paperback)
ISBN 9798892135559 (ebook)
Subjects: LCSH: Artificial intelligence at home | Home automation—Juvenile literature. | Artificial intelligence—Juvenile literature.
Classification: LCC TK7881.25 .M33 2025 (print)
LCC TK7881.25 (ebook)
DDC 643/.6028563—dc23/eng/20240708
LC record available at https://lccn.loc.gov/2024023292
LC ebook record available at https://lccn.loc.gov/202

Editor: Alyssa Sorenson
Designer: Emma Almgren-Bersie

Photo Credits: Oliver Hasselluhn/iStock, cover; Bet_Noire/iStock, 1; Svetlana Mahovskaya/Shutterstock, 3; Pixel-Shot/Shutterstock, 4; InFocus.ee/Shutterstock, 5 (foreground); Kues/Shutterstock, 5 (background); RichLegg/iStock, 6-7; South_agency/iStock, 8-9; HenadziPechan/Shutterstock, 10; fetrinka/Shutterstock, 11; years44/Shutterstock, 12-13; Plan Shooting 2/Imazins/Getty, 14-15; onurdongel/iStock, 16; Janis Abolins/Shutterstock, 17; fcafotodigital/iStock, 18-19; iLexx/iStock, 20-21; Mariia Vitkovska/iStock, 21; Kirillm/iStock, 23.

Printed in the United States of America at Corporate Graphics in North Mankato, Minnesota.

TABLE OF CONTENTS

CHAPTER 1
What Is AI?...4

CHAPTER 2
The Smart Home...10

CHAPTER 3
Smart Homes of the Future......................16

ACTIVITIES & TOOLS
Try This!...22
Glossary...23
Index...24
To Learn More...24

CHAPTER 1
WHAT IS AI?

A **robot** vacuum cleans the floor. It has **sensors**. It notices a couch leg in its way. It moves around it. It remembers where the couch is for next time!

robot vacuum

This is an example of **artificial intelligence** (AI). AI programs help computers and machines learn and make decisions. AI does things humans use knowledge to do.

CHAPTER 1 5

We can use AI in many ways at home. Like what? Smart **appliances** use AI to help us cook. Smart cameras recognize faces at your front door. Smart **devices** make our lives easier!

DID YOU KNOW?

Many smart devices use **Wi-Fi**. Why? This connects them to the internet. They get information for you. Ask a smart speaker when your favorite TV star was born. It looks it up online. It tells you!

Smart devices communicate. How? They connect to each other using **Bluetooth**. A smart phone or speaker sends commands to other smart devices. For example, you can use a phone app to tell a robot vacuum to start.

CHAPTER 1

TAKE A LOOK!

How do devices connect in a smart home? Take a look!

A robot vacuum starts.

A smart light turns on.

Devices connect to a smart phone. A person uses apps on their phone. The devices respond!

A smart thermostat changes the home's temperature.

CHAPTER 1

CHAPTER 2
THE SMART HOME

Look around. What is smart in your home? Robots that use AI can do **chores**. Some clean windows.

window cleaning robot

Others mow the lawn. AI helps robots find the best path. How? Sensors look for grass. They also find rocks in the way. The robots use AI to understand what the sensors notice. Then the robots use AI to decide where to go.

AI understands language. Smart speakers wait for a voice command. When they hear it, they turn on. People talk to smart speakers. They use them to shop online. They ask what the weather is like. They tell the speaker to turn off the lights. Smart speakers do much more!

DID YOU KNOW?

A smart speaker records when you talk. Why? It figures out what you need. But it may accidentally record private talks. The company that made the device can hear.

CHAPTER 2

Smart appliances do a lot, too. Can't decide what to make for dinner? A smart fridge can help! It knows what food is inside. It searches online. It comes up with **recipes**.

DID YOU KNOW?

Smart ovens with AI help you cook. How? They learn how to tell when food is done. You do not need to set a timer. Your food won't burn!

CHAPTER 2   15

CHAPTER 3
SMART HOMES OF THE FUTURE

New AI **technology** is created all the time. Many people like how useful it is. They add more smart devices to their homes.

Future AI could help us use electricity in smarter ways. It could know to keep empty rooms cooler. It could turn off lights in those rooms, too. These smart actions save electricity. This helps the **environment**.

CHAPTER 3   17

AI can also reduce waste. Smart fridges keep track of when food will go bad. The fridge could suggest how to use the food.

CHAPTER 3

CHAPTER 3

Today, each robot has its own purpose. But someday, one robot could do many things. Maybe it will use AI to do all of your chores. It might learn to mow the lawn. It could run a dishwasher. It could wash your clothes. What could AI do in your home?

ACTIVITIES & TOOLS

TRY THIS!

CREATE NEW AI TECHNOLOGY

How would AI be useful in your home? Come up with new ideas with this fun activity!

What You Need:
- paper and pencil or a device for taking notes

1. Look around your home. Does your family have devices or appliances that use AI? Make a list of them.
2. Make a list of family chores. Does a smart device or appliance help with any of them?
3. Choose one chore that does not use AI. Think about how AI could make that chore easier or faster.
4. Create new AI. Is it an appliance, a robot, or another device? What does your technology do? Write down your ideas. Share them with a friend or family member.

GLOSSARY

appliances: Machines that do specific jobs, like ovens or vacuum cleaners.

artificial intelligence: The science of making computers do things that previously needed human intelligence, such as understanding language.

Bluetooth: A technology that connects devices that are close to each other without using wires.

chores: Jobs around the home that have to be done regularly, such as cleaning.

devices: Electronic objects that do specific jobs.

environment: The natural surroundings of living things, such as the air, land, or ocean.

recipes: Instructions for preparing food.

robot: A machine that is programmed to perform complex human tasks.

sensors: Tools that notice and measure changes for a device.

technology: The use of science and engineering to do practical things.

Wi-Fi: A wireless signal that lets devices connect to the internet without wires.

ACTIVITIES & TOOLS

INDEX

app 8, 9
appliances 7, 15
Bluetooth 8
cameras 7
chores 10, 21
commands 8, 12
devices 7, 8, 9, 12, 16
electricity 17
environment 17
internet 7
language 12
light 9, 12, 17

mow 11, 21
programs 5
recipes 15
records 12
robot 4, 8, 9, 10, 11, 21
sensors 4, 11
shop 12
speaker 7, 8, 12
thermostat 9
vacuum 4, 8, 9
waste 18
Wi-Fi 7

TO LEARN MORE

Finding more information is as easy as 1, 2, 3.

❶ Go to www.factsurfer.com
❷ Enter "Alathome" into the search box.
❸ Choose your book to see a list of websites.

24 ACTIVITIES & TOOLS